Should We Have Faith in Central Banks?

Should We Have Faith in Central Banks?

OTMAR ISSING

WITH A COMMENTARY BY GEOFFREY E. WOOD

The Institute of Economic Affairs

First published in Great Britain in 2002 by
The Institute of Economic Affairs
2 Lord North Street
Westminster
London SW1P 3LB
in association with Profile Books Ltd

A CIP catalogue record for this book is available from the British Library.

ISBN 0 255 36528 4

Many IEA publications are translated into languages other than English or are
reprinted. Permission to translate or to reprint should be sought from the
General Director at the address above.

Typeset in Stone by MacGuru
info@macguru.org.uk

Printed and bound in Great Britain by Hobbs the Printers

CONTENTS

THE AUTHORS

Otmar Issing

Professor Otmar Issing, who was born in 1936, has been a member of the Executive Board of the European Central Bank since 1 June 1998. The business areas for which he is responsible include the Directorates General Economics and Research. Until May 1998 he was a member of the board of the Deutsche Bundesbank with a seat on the Central Bank Council. Prior to that he held chairs of economics at the universities of Würzburg and Erlangen-Nürnberg. In 1991 he was awarded an honorary professorship at the University of Würzburg. From 1988 to 1990 he was a member of the German Council of Experts for the Assessment of Overall Economic Developments. He is an active member of the Akademie der Wissenschaften und der Literatur (Academy of Sciences and Literature), Mainz, and of the Academia Scientiarum et Artium Europaea (European Academy of Sciences and Arts). In addition to publishing numerous articles in scientific journals and periodicals, he is the author of, *inter alia*, two textbooks, *Einführung in die Geldtheorie* (Introduction to Monetary Theory), twelfth edition 2001, and *Einführung in die Geldpolitik* (Introduction to Monetary Policy), sixth edition 1996.

Geoffrey E. Wood

Geoffrey E. Wood is Professor of Economics at City University Business School, London. He has also taught at the University of Warwick, and has been on the research staff of the Bank of England and the Federal Reserve Bank of St Louis. He has published extensively in the areas of monetary economics and international economics. Among his publications are (for the IEA) *Too Much Money?*, written with Gordon T. Pepper (Hobart Paper 68, 1975); *Central Bank Independence: What Is It and What Will It Do For Us?*, written with Forrest Capie and Terence Mills (Current Controversies 4, 1993); and *The Right Road to Monetary Union Revisited*, written with John Chown and Massimo Beber (Current Controversies 8, 1994). He is a Trustee of the Institute of Economic Affairs and of the Wincott Foundation.

FOREWORD

The move towards central bank independence in recent years, which has taken place mainly because of concern in many countries about the politicisation of monetary policy, has placed considerable power in the hands of central bankers. But why should they be trusted to exercise that power for the benefit of the community as a whole?

In Occasional Paper 125, this question is addressed by Professor Otmar Issing, a leading monetary economist and one of Europe's most influential central bankers. Professor Issing has previously written for the IEA, both on central bank independence and on the European single currency.[1] In this new paper, which is a revised and extended version of a lecture he gave in Cambridge, he poses the problem directly:

> There is today a broad consensus that stable money is too important to be left to the day-to-day political process ... it makes sense for society to create an independent institution that stands above the fray of day-to-day politics and can pursue this objective [price stability] with minimum distraction.

However, 'why should one trust central bankers more than

---

1   *Central Bank Independence and Monetary Stability*, Occasional Paper 89, 1993; *Europe: Political Union through Common Money*, Occasional Paper 98, 1996; and *Hayek, Currency Competition and European Monetary Union*, Occasional Paper 111, 2000.

politicians?' Should there not be rules – such as Milton Friedman's proposal for a constitutional rule of constant money growth – to avoid the need to place trust in a particular group of people?

Issing's answer is that an independent central bank with a 'clear and limited mandate' represents a constraint on the discretionary use of power by either the central bank or government. In other words, the independent central bank itself represents a set of rules: it is a means of reducing '... reliance on faith in the wisdom and moral virtue of individuals in the pursuit of desirable objectives'.

Taking the responsibility for the 'common good of price stability' outside partisan politics and giving the central bank freedom to pursue its mandate make sense, says Issing, but the bank, as agent, must be accountable to its principal, the public. In the case of the European Central Bank (ECB), its price stability aim is enshrined in an international treaty which confers democratic legitimacy. Explicit performance contracts for central bankers are one way of providing incentives but, Professor Issing points out, such contracts must always be incomplete – it is impossible to specify in advance all possible contingencies, so monitoring performance is not straightforward.

Professor Issing comments also on the nature of monetary union in Europe, which is unprecedented in history and has severed '... the traditionally close link between the currency and the nation state'. In his view

> ... European economic and monetary union has been and will continue to be part of the wider economic and political project that the process of European integration has represented from the very start.

He concludes that central bankers have no right to expect blind faith from the public. They operate best in institutions that have a clear objective and which are held accountable by the public. They must build up trust in 'solid and strong independent institutions which are dedicated to serving and defending the common good of price stability'.

Professor Geoffrey Wood, of City University Business School, in a commentary on Professor Issing's paper, puts it in the context of the 'rules versus discretion' debate begun by Henry Simons, and then deals with three issues related to those in the paper.

First, he points to the problem of measuring the rate of price change, which means that it is not possible to be certain what 'price stability' means. Technical change, which leads to improvements in the quality of goods, is generally believed to result in the over-estimation of inflation by consumer price indices. Thus, both the Bank of England and the ECB have inflation targets that are above zero (1.5 to 3.5 per cent and less than 2 per cent, respectively) but which are thought to approximate to stable prices.

Second, he deals with the role of stable money if the economy is to function well. Unless money has a predictable value, price signals are muted and a market economy can easily be undermined. So the performance of a central bank with a price stability goal is critical to the operation of a market economy.

Third, he argues that central banks must maintain financial stability as well as monetary stability. It is not possible to lay down rigid rules for a central bank as lender of last resort, so there must be trust that the bank will act quickly and vigorously, should a crisis arise.

As in all Institute publications, the views expressed are those of the authors, not of the Institute (which has no corporate view), its managing trustees, Academic Advisory Council members or senior staff. The paper by Professor Issing and the commentary by Professor Wood are published as contributions to the lively discussions now in train about the role of central banks and ways of ensuring that their power is not abused.

COLIN ROBINSON

Editorial Director, Institute of Economic Affairs
Professor of Economics, University of Surrey
April 2002

SUMMARY

- Stable prices are the foundation of a well-functioning market economy.
- There is a broad consensus that stable money is '... too important to be left to the day-to-day political process'.
- Stable money is a common good and it makes sense to create an independent institution that can pursue this good with minimum distraction. That is the basis for central bank independence.
- A central bank with a 'clear and limited mandate' represents a set of rules that constrain the discretionary use of power by the government or the central bank. It is a more flexible solution in the setting of monetary policy than mechanical rules.
- Central banks are agents for their principals, the public, and they need to be accountable. A clear and limited mandate simplifies the problem of accountability to the public.
- The European Central Bank (ECB) has its price stability objective enshrined in an international treaty, so providing democratic legitimacy.
- Performance contracts for central bankers are one way of providing appropriate incentives but, in practice, complete contracts cannot be specified and performance is hard to monitor.

- European economic and monetary union is part of a wider economic and political project.
- People should not have blind faith in central bankers, who perform best in an institution with a clear objective that is held accountable to the public.
- In his commentary, Geoffrey Wood adds that price stability, though essential to the proper functioning of markets, is difficult to measure because of technical change. Central banks also have a responsibility to maintain financial stability.

Should We Have Faith in Central Banks?

SHOULD WE HAVE FAITH IN CENTRAL BANKS?[1]

A look at the dictionary

Should we have faith in central banks? My answer to this question depends on what is meant by 'faith'. A natural starting point is to take a look at the dictionary. The term 'faith' is used in a religious context as well as in everyday language. From the Concise Oxford Dictionary[2] I derive three main uses of the term 'faith'. These different meanings are also reflected in the history of philosophical approaches to faith and belief.[3]

First, there is the theological meaning of faith as 'belief in religious doctrine', 'spiritual apprehension of divine truth apart from proof' or, more generally, 'belief founded on authority'. Here, Blaise Pascal springs to mind as an advocate of a strict separation between faith and reason. In his view one could not arrive at faith by means of reasoning but only 'through the heart'.

On this first definition my answer to the question posed by the

---

1   This is a revised and extended version of the Millennium Lecture given at St Edmund's College, Cambridge, on 26 October 2000 as a contribution to a series of lectures on the general theme 'Faith in the Future'. I would like to thank Bernhard Winkler for his valuable contribution.

2   The Concise Oxford Dictionary, 7th ed., Oxford University Press, Oxford, 1982.

3   For what follows see the entry under *'Glaube'* (faith) in J. Ritter (ed.), *Historisches Wörterbuch der Philosophie*, Wissenschaftliche Buchgesellschaft Darmstadt, vol. 3, Basel, 1974, with extensive references.

title of my lecture is 'no'. I would prefer to confine faith, in the sense of unquestioned belief, strictly to the private and religious sphere. When it comes to central banking neither the central bankers' actions nor the public's expectations can afford just to rely on faith devoid of proof or evidence. Moreover, I do not regard it as helpful to characterise central banking as some sort of mystical art that aims to instil awe and worship. On the contrary, I consider that the public would be generally ill advised to place 'blind trust' in particular individuals or institutions. This is an important lesson to take away from liberal economic and political philosophy, as well as from the overwhelming merits of the democratic system of government. Ultimately, trust must be earned, it is granted temporarily, it must be checked, and it must be backed up by hard evidence, not be based purely on faith or belief.

Second, faith is used in everyday language as a synonym for 'belief', 'reliance' and 'trust', which could perhaps be interpreted in the sense of 'well-founded expectation'. In this context one could think of faith as a probabilistic statement. Immanuel Kant has associated faith with an intermediate degree of certainty, more than mere 'opinion' but short of 'knowledge'.

On this definition my basic answer to the question becomes 'yes'. At least in the example of the institution I represent, I see good reasons for believing that the public in Europe can have such faith, and that it can rely on the European Central Bank (ECB) to fulfil its mandate and maintain price stability. This sort of 'reasoned faith' or 'confidence' is (as it should be) underpinned by a sound institutional set-up, the application of well-established economic principles and, last but not least, by the quality and determination of the people dedicated to this task.

A third aspect of faith relates to 'keeping a promise' or 'engagement', as in 'acting in good faith', in the sense of reflecting 'honesty of intention'. For Thomas Hobbes 'to have faith', 'to trust' and 'to believe a man' are synonymous. One could think of this dimension of faith as representing a two-sided relationship, rather than a unilateral act of faith.

From this perspective faith – or, better here, trust – is similar to a contract established between two parties. The faith that the public places in the central bank imposes a constant obligation on the central bank to honour this trust and fulfil the promise of stable money. The bond of trust between the public and its central bank can be seen as something like a credit relationship. Indeed, the term 'credit' is Latin for 'he believes'; that is, it expresses the hope and expectation that initially one-sided trust will be reciprocated and returned in the future. Trust is given 'on credit' but in turn it is based on credibility or trustworthiness.

If you allow me to jump from these etymological reflections straight to the mundane tasks of central banking in practice, I would like to stress the following. In the case of European Monetary Union the promise of maintaining stable prices – and thus maintaining the value of money – is built on solid and credible institutional foundations. So far in its young life the European Central Bank has lived up to its promise, and there is every reason to believe that price stability in the euro area will continue to be maintained over the medium term. Long-term bond yields and surveys of inflation expectations continue to indicate a high degree of confidence in the ECB's ability to deliver on its primary objective over the medium term. This is what ultimately counts. For this achievement the ECB can deservedly claim some 'credit'.

In the remainder of the lecture I will concentrate mainly on trust and credibility as two aspects of 'faith' that appear most relevant for monetary policy-making. Trust and the quest for credibility are at the core of a monetary economy, the role of central banks in such an economy and the search for an appropriate monetary constitution. This is not to say that there is no room for faith as 'belief based on authority', both in the public perception of central banks and of central bankers.

Trust: the role of money and the value of price stability

One does not have to look very far in order to find a link between faith and money. In fact, every one-dollar bill bears the inscription 'In God we trust'. The euro is more secular in this respect. In the case of sterling, the pound notes feature a 'promise to pay the bearer' of the note the amount stated. This points to the very nature of money as being built on trust, on a promise. Trust is crucial for money to function as a medium of exchange, as a store of value and as a stable unit of account. Using economic terminology, money – or rather the trust that underpins the use of money – has public-good characteristics or confers positive network externalities on all participants in the economy. In this way money economises significantly on the costs of transactions that would be present in a pure barter economy.

If you look more closely at the dollar bill, you will find a further inscription which states 'This note is legal tender for all debt, public and private'. This imposes an obligation to accept the note in the settlement of contracts and highlights the fact that money derives its value – whether imposed by a legal tender requirement or not – from the willingness of other economic agents to accept it to settle transactions. Each agent will only accept money if he can be confident that it will in turn be accepted by other agents in future transactions. Thus money is a social achievement, as has long been recognised by economists, for example by Carl Menger. Money is a question of trust, its use requires trust and it reflects trust. This is especially true in the case of fiat money; that is, the use of printed paper – which has no intrinsic worth – as a medium of exchange and as a store of value. Yet even commodity money requires trust and a well-founded expectation that it will be accepted for a wide range of transactions.

Milton Friedman, in his book *Money Mischief*,[4] reports the well-known story of the monetary system of a small island in Micronesia which at the end of the nineteenth century used stone wheels as a medium of exchange and as a store of wealth. He recounts an episode when the colonial government imposed 'fees' on disobedient district chiefs simply by painting black crosses on these stone wheels. This miraculously and promptly induced them to change their ways just in order to have these marks erased again and thus – in their perception – their wealth restored. Friedman concludes that this example illustrates 'how important appearance or illusion or "myth", given unquestioned belief, becomes in monetary matters. Our own money, the money we have grown up with, the system under which it is controlled, these appear "real" and "rational" to us. Yet the money of other countries often seems to us like paper or worthless metal, even when the purchasing power of individual units is quite high.'

The euro has been in existence for over three years now. It does not come in the form of stone wheels. In fact, until the beginning of 2002 it did not have any concrete and tangible expression at all.

---

4   M. Friedman, *Money Mischief – Episodes in Monetary History*, Harcourt Brace Jovanovich, New York, 1992, pp. 3–7.

Until the introduction of euro banknotes and coins at the beginning of 2002 it remained a 'virtual' currency, which perhaps seemed as remote, unfamiliar and unnatural in the eyes of the public as the stone wheels described by Friedman. This lack of tangibility and visibility of the euro compounded the particular challenges that the euro faces in winning the hearts of the general public as a new currency replacing the familiar and trusted national notes and coins in circulation. As Friedman's example shows, symbols may be important in monetary matters. At the same time, irrespective of the particular symbols and media to which money functions are attached – be it stone wheels or computer chips – money is ultimately a question of trust. The euro's existence until recently as a 'non-tangible currency' perhaps makes this point – which is valid for any fiat money – more plain and obvious.

No matter what specific medium of exchange a society might wish to adopt, the efficiency of money in facilitating economic transactions via the price mechanism depends on its stability as a unit of account – that is, as a common financial denominator – for the economy. In order to hold and accept money, economic agents must not only be confident that money remains accepted as a medium for exchange, but also be confident that money will retain its value over time, thereby ensuring that price signals can provide accurate guidance for markets to function efficiently. In contrast, if money loses its value, this also undermines its usefulness for exchange. Indeed, in periods of very high inflation currency tends to be replaced, for example, by cigarettes or other goods – or, perhaps, 'bads' – in everyday transactions. An inflationary currency will simply cease to be accepted in transactions, notwithstanding any legal-tender provisions such as those written on the dollar bills. I am old enough to remember such a period in post-war Germany, before the currency reform of 1948.

Stable money, stable prices: these are the very foundations of a well-functioning market economy. There is a strong economic case for price stability, which today is – again – widely accepted. However, the case for price stability goes beyond the purely economic sphere. Price stability, the ability to rely on stable money, is the basis for trust in the interaction among economic agents, trust in property rights, trust in society and trust in the future more generally. Trust in stable money is also the basis for a free society, the ability of people to take decisions and plan their future for themselves. This is particularly evident with respect to lifetime savings for retirement, which is a topical issue at the moment in the context of discussions over a greater role for private pension schemes. Private provision of retirement savings crucially requires the trust of savers in the long-run stability of money. Conversely, a loss of such confidence inevitably leads to calls on the state to step in and provide for the future collectively. Inflation undermines trust in money and in property rights more generally. This mechanism was apparently recognised by Lenin, who allegedly remarked that the 'most effective way to destroy civil society is to destroy its money'.[5]

There is a saying that 'peace is not everything, but without peace everything else comes to nothing'. I am tempted to say the same thing for price stability.

Inflation – like war, with which it is often closely associated – destroys the fruit of honest labour, it devalues savings and invest-

---

5   Attributed to Lenin in W. Eucken, *Grundsätze der Wirtschaftspolitik*, 2nd ed., Mohr, Tübingen, 1955, p. 255.

ment, it erodes the social fabric of society and, ultimately, puts the very foundations of democracy and freedom at risk. This is one of the lessons of the bitter history of the twentieth century, which was a century of hyperinflation in the wake of wars and wars in the wake of hyperinflation. No one has described the deleterious effects of inflation more vividly than Stefan Zweig has done in his book *Die Welt von Gestern* on Germany in the 1920s. He depicts the sense of distrust, despondency, desolation and despair that hyperinflation brought to Germany in 1923 (in the wake of World War I), from which the fragile democratic and economic institutions of the young republic were never really to recover (thus preparing the ground for World War II).

Zweig contrasts this with the pre-war 'golden age of security', when 'it paid to put money year for year in safe investments', when 'the saver was not yet robbed', the 'honest deceived', but when the 'most patient, not the speculators, had the greatest profit'. He concludes 'that nothing has rendered the German people so embittered, so full of hatred, so ready for Hitler as this inflation' (own translation).[6]

From this one could establish not just an economic case but also an ethical obligation to maintain price stability. Indeed, as far back as the Middle Ages Nicolaus Oresme argued in favour of stable money as a principle of natural law and denounced the debasing of currency by the state as worse than usury and equivalent to robbery and exploitation.[7] In our times another bishop, Karl Lehmann, the current chair of the German Conference of Bishops, has stressed a moral and ethical justification for price stability. In

---

6   S. Zweig, *Die Welt von Gestern*, Frankfurt am Main, 1955, p. 359.

7   N. Oresme, *Traktat über Geldabwertungen*, ed. E. Schorer, Verlag Gustav Fischer, Jena, 1937, p. 63.

line with recent documents of Catholic social teaching, he empha-
sises that inflation tends to hit the weakest segments of the popu-
lation hardest and that it has contributed to impoverishment, in
particular in developing countries.[8]

On the whole, however, the world of faith and the world of
money eye each other with a good measure of distrust and suspi-
cion. Men of faith have often regarded money as the symbol of
greed, sin and evil rather than as an instrument for mutually beneficial exchange and a foundation of prosperity. The Christian ethical tradition has in particular expressed moral reservations about
the trading or lending of money against an interest charge. This
sceptical attitude towards money and charging interest, which to
an economist is simply the intertemporal price of money, was well
entrenched in the Scholastic tradition and goes back to Aristotle's
view that to 'make money out of money' would go against natural
law. Interestingly, such moral scruples on lending against interest
are also found in other religions, and this form of lending is banned
to this day in the Islamic world. I must admit that, as a central
banker charged with setting official interest rates, I have difficul-
ties in accepting this particular – to my mind unfounded – belief,
even if the authority in question is claimed to be Aristotle or the
Bible, both of which I am quite happy to consult on other matters.

Credibility: the role of rules and institutions

The weight of historical experience and a large body of theoretical

---

8   K. Lehmann, 'Geld – Segen oder Mammon? Biblische Aspekte – Ein Arbeits-
     papier', in H. Hesse and O. Issing (eds), *Geld und Moral*, München, 1994,
     pp. 125–37.

literature and of empirical evidence point to the importance of price stability as the foundation of a well-functioning market economy and as a pre-condition for durable growth and prosperity. Nevertheless history is littered with episodes of high inflation which imposed high economic and social costs on society. To be sure, at times the importance of the common and precious good of price stability may have been underrated or forgotten by society. At other times stability may have been purposefully compromised in the pursuit of other seemingly more pressing objectives. However, the main lesson that I would take away from history is this: when it comes to price stability, good faith and honest intentions are not enough.

Fundamentally, money represents a promise. It requires trust on the part of the users of money that the issuer of money will honour this promise. Money is built on trust, but in turn trust must be built on solid foundations. The promise must be made credible and this – at least in relatively modern times – is the job of central bankers.

A promise always concerns the future. As we know when we make promises in everyday life, when the time comes to make good on our promises there is a danger that we find either our mind or the situation has changed. Perhaps we may simply have forgotten what we said in the past or would like to change our plans under the pressure of a myriad of more pressing concerns. This is all very human. It also describes the core of the much-discussed problem of credibility in monetary policy. Thus a good monetary constitution that can be expected durably to deliver on the promise of stability needs to take human frailty and imperfection into account. As elsewhere in public life, in monetary policy one should not and cannot simply rely on good intentions, blind trust or unquestioned authority.

Can we trust central banks and can we expect them to be credible in making good on their promise of price stability?

There is today a broad consensus that stable money is too important to be left to the day-to-day political process, which inevitably will always have to balance different objectives, conflicting interests and short-term pressures. If stable money is regarded as a common good for the benefit of all, and if it is seen as a pre-condition for long-term prosperity and social justice, then it makes sense for society to create an independent institution that stands above the fray of day-to-day politics and can pursue this objective with minimum distraction. This is the basis for central bank independence.

If price stability, by contrast, were regarded as just one of a long list of political and economic objectives – rather than as a common goal and a pre-condition for the successful pursuit of other objectives – then there would be no legitimacy for entrusting this task (and only this task) to independent central banks. Making value judgements when trading off different objectives and balancing conflicting interests is the legitimate job of elected politicians with a popular mandate, and not of appointed technocrats.

An independent central bank thus presupposes a broad consensus on the 'quasi-constitutional' nature of the common good of price stability. Assigning the central bank a clear overriding objective also imposes limits on its discretionary exercise of power and makes it easier for the public to hold the central bank accountable for its mandate. It is important to keep this in mind if we entertain the possibility that while 'money is too important to be left to the politicians' one could similarly concur with Milton Friedman, who (citing Poincaré) maintains that 'money is too important to be left to central bankers'.[9] In other words, why should one trust central bankers more than politicians?

Friedman, at least at the time he wrote, trusted neither of the two, and advocated a constitutional rule for constant money growth as his favoured solution to the long-standing debate on 'Rules versus authorities in monetary policy' (which is the title of the classic paper by Henry Simons in 1936[10]). His concerns reflect what I would regard as a healthy distrust of the unfettered 'rule of men' as opposed to the 'rule of law', which he much prefers – in line with the long and venerable tradition of British liberal thinking. Friedman, at the time, was quite sceptical about central bank independence and asked whether it was 'really tolerable in a democracy to have so much power concentrated in a body free from any kind of direct, effective political control'.

That is why I believe it is important to stress that, if an independent central bank is assigned a clear and limited mandate, this represents a constraint on the discretionary exercise of power not only by the government but also by the central bank itself. In the absence of a complete and universally applicable rule for monetary policy, an independent central bank which is firmly committed to the single overriding goal of price stability is the closest realistic and credible approximation to a literal 'rule of law'. In particular, such a central bank does not have the discretion to pick and choose at will among several objectives.

Institutions, such as central banks, themselves represent sets of rules. They are a way of reducing reliance on faith in the wisdom

---

9   M. Friedman, 'Should there be an independent monetary authority?', in L.B. Yeager (ed.), *In Search of a Monetary Constitution*, Cambridge, Mass., 1962.

10 H.C. Simons, 'Rules versus Authorities in Monetary Policy?', *Journal of Political Economy*, vol. 44, pp. 1–30.

and moral virtue of individuals in the pursuit of desirable objectives. Institutions delineate the power of individuals and limit their discretion in the exercise of power. Appropriately designed and independent institutions thus offer an alternative form of commitment to overcome credibility problems. At the same time the institutional solution of an independent central bank allows for greater flexibility than the adoption of any strict mechanical rule for setting monetary policy. Such a strict rule would in any case be difficult to implement and enforce. As Friedman himself acknowledged, in the 1962 essay quoted earlier, one 'cannot dispense fully with the rule of men' since 'no law can be specified so precisely as to avoid problems of interpretation or to cover explicitly every case'.

This implies that individual judgement will still matter in the conduct of monetary policy and also in the monitoring of monetary policy by the public. Institutions are obviously made up of and led by individuals – within the rules set by the institution – on whom the quality of decision-making will depend. Thus even the most properly designed institutions require the right choice of individuals at their helm and that the right choices be made by those individuals. This suggests that in the end 'faith' in institutions such as central banks and 'faith' in the individuals in charge of these institutions often cannot be easily distinguished. But 'faith' with respect to which attributes of individual decision-makers? What matters most, surely, in the case of central bankers is their competence, their ability to fulfil their public function and the mandate they have been entrusted with. Within the constraints and incentives of a well-defined institutional setting one need rely much less on individual ethical behaviour. What counts is the technical competence and professional skills of the central banker.

Delegating authority and placing trust in institutions that are assigned a clear objective thus seem preferable to relying solely on the discretion and good faith of individuals, on the one hand, and imposing strict mechanical rules on the other hand. An institution may be made up of individuals. But an institution is also more than the mere sum of individuals. That is the very reason for the existence of institutions – otherwise there would be no need for them. Institutions instil and reflect a sense of common purpose and responsibility. They provide discipline and guidance for individual behaviour within such an institution. They provide support and strength to the individuals making up the institution. As a consequence, institutions are more reliable and more durable carriers of trust and reputation than individuals alone. The strength of an institutional approach is particularly evident in the case of independent central banks.

Central bank independence and accountability

Accountability is the reverse side of the coin of independence. As explained above, it makes good economic sense to take the responsibility for the common good of price stability outside the direct, day-to-day influence of partisan politics. It is also perfectly democratically legitimate for society to delegate authority for a particular policy area to an institution outside the regular political process. Granting such decision-making authority to an independent central bank, in a democracy, means that the central bank must assume the responsibility for its use of this authority. Central bank independence requires accountability. However, the reverse is also true. Central banks can only be held accountable if they are fully free and independent in taking decisions related to their mandate. A clear division of responsibilities between the central bank, on the one hand, and the government and legislature, on the other hand, is therefore a pre-condition for effective accountability.

It is sometimes argued that there is a conflict or a trade-off between accountability, on the one hand, and the independence and credibility of central banks on the other hand. I do not share this view. Quite the contrary – accountability and central bank independence go hand in hand if the central bank is given a clear and limited mandate. This requires a consensus that price stability is a common good that should not be and must not be subject to the normal kinds of trade-offs and value judgements that are the domain of the regular political process. A clear and limited mandate is thus the basis for central bank independence.

A clear and limited mandate also sharpens the incentives and the focus for monetary policy and thus provides the basis for central bank credibility. Finally, a clear and limited mandate makes it easier for the public to hold the central bank accountable. This, in turn, should enhance performance incentives and credibility further. If monetary policy were instead to be called upon to serve a multitude of – usually competing – goals, the status of independence would be both much harder to justify and the related accountability much more difficult to achieve.

In the case of the ECB, the primary objective of maintaining price stability is enshrined in an international treaty, which would be rather difficult to change. Its quasi-constitutional character, while offering greater protection from political interference, does not mean that the ECB's mandate carries less democratic legitimacy. On the contrary, a treaty concluded by fifteen national governments and ratified by fifteen national parliaments, in some cases endorsed in addition by a popular referendum, confers a robust degree of democratic legitimacy. Once it is accepted that price stability is a lasting value and not simply a short-term objective, it appears fully justified that the ECB, as the institution entrusted with maintaining price stability, should be afforded a high degree of legal protection in the pursuit of this objective.

There can be no doubt that an independent central bank should and must be held accountable for the achievement of the mandate it has been entrusted with – and only for that mandate. The question is how such accountability can best be implemented and to whom it should refer. In a democracy accountability must ultimately be achieved vis-à-vis the supreme sovereign – that is, the people whose interests the institution must serve. In this relationship the public acts as the principal who delegates the task of monetary policy to the central bank as its agent in order to achieve a well-specified objective. The act of delegation can be one-off, of a constitutional nature, or it can be periodically renewed. In both cases the central bank needs to be held accountable for its performance by the public. However, this can be achieved in different – more or less formal – ways.

Depending on the specific institutional context and traditions, such accountability to the public is often intermediated and implemented in the form of reporting requirements vis-à-vis parliament as well as the general public. When the central bank's objective is set by the government, accountability may also involve the executive in some form. This is not the case for the ECB, whose mandate is given by treaty. This mandate is a European one. As far as monetary policy is concerned the locus of accountability of the ECB can therefore only be at the European level. Thus the ECB is accountable vis-à-vis the European public and its elected representatives in the European Parliament.

Explicit performance contracts for central bankers have been suggested as one way of providing appropriate incentives, enhancing accountability and credibility and reducing the reliance on trust in individual ethical behaviour. For example, salaries of central bank governors could be linked in some way to the measured inflation rate, or the governors could be dismissed if a certain inflation threshold is reached. An explicit contractual approach to accountability requires that the assessment of performance be based on easily observable and verifiable elements in the decision-making process. However, there are limits to the extent to which the behaviour of individuals inside an institution can be monitored and verified precisely from the outside. Thus explicit performance contracts would in practice have to be simple and crude. They would have to be based on observed economic outcomes, which are affected by the decisions only after a considerable time lag. Moreover, the outcome will at any point in time also be affected by many other intervening influences outside the control of the central bank.

The basic difficulty with a formal, contractual approach is the one pointed out already by Friedman. It will in general not be possible to specify a written contract that can cover all possible contingencies and which could be verified unambiguously *ex post*. Furthermore, in cases where decision-making is undertaken by committee – as is the case for the majority of independent central banks – it might be rather difficult to disentangle individual contributions and responsibilities with respect to the common decisions taken. For these reasons accountability may have to be achieved in less formal and explicit ways and applied to the relationship between the public and the central bank as an institution, rather than primarily with respect to individual central bankers.

However, even if no explicit contractual elements and specific sanctions are incorporated in this relationship, the delegation of decision-making authority to an independent central bank establishes a kind of quasi-contractual relationship. The delegation of authority represents an act of trust on the part of the public and it represents a promise and an obligation on the part of the central bank to fulfil its mandate.

The strength of an institutional approach combining elements of implicit and explicit contracts, formal and informal sets of rules, and combining individual and collective responsibility is particularly evident in the case of independent central banks. In the context of monetary policy-making there are particular merits in decision-making by committee. On the one hand, this allows diverse experiences, arguments and points of views to be brought to the table, thus reducing the risk of policy errors. On the other hand, there is a shared responsibility for the common decisions taken. It is not a single individual but the entire institution that is behind these decisions. To my mind both aspects are crucial for a strong, independent and credible central bank.

So, should we – should you – have faith in central banks? The answer is yes and no. *No*, it would not be wise always and everywhere to trust *central bankers* with our money, but, *yes*, there are good reasons for trusting *central banks*, if they are designed as solid and independent institutions with a clearly defined mandate. Institutions limit the faith we need to place in the omniscience and benevolence of individual decision-makers and provide a more lasting and reliable basis for trust and credibility.

Faith and reputation: the role of central banks in society

Properly designed institutions provide the basis for trust and confidence. However, this trust must be earned, maintained and confirmed through action over time. Like individuals, institutions become carriers of reputation as a function of their past behaviour. This reputation forms the basis for expectations of future behaviour.

In the case of the European Central Bank, the institutional preconditions for credible and successful monetary policy are in place. The ECB is built on trustworthy institutional foundations. As a new institution, however, it started out without a track record and thus cannot rely on an established reputation. The statutes and institutional set-up of the ECB have worked very well to date and the Governing Council has taken its monetary policy decisions in full independence. However, firmly to establish trust and reputation takes time. Trust is deepened and reputation is built when it is tested in difficult circumstances and when it is maintained over an extended period. Until a sufficient track record is established, the ECB – by necessity – has to rely primarily on the strength of its institutional set-up and the force of its arguments to win the trust of the public.

It is unsurprising that, as a new institution, the ECB has been subject to an extraordinary degree of public scrutiny and indeed criticism in its young life. I firmly believe that over time this is generally a healthy situation. Over time any public institution that is based on a sound constitutional foundation can only benefit from being open to outside advice and from being exposed to criticism and debate. This creates desirable incentives for constant improvement and helps the institution to strengthen its commitment to fulfil its mandate in the best possible way. An open, frank and fair dialogue is particularly crucial in the process of developing understanding and a bond of trust between a young institution like the ECB and its principal, whom it ultimately serves – that is, the European public. I believe that this process of trust-building requires some patience and indeed 'good faith' on both sides. Not 'blind faith', but perhaps some 'goodwill'.

Undoubtedly, well-established central banks with a long and proud history like the Bank of England, the Federal Reserve or the Bundesbank face an easier task in this regard. They can draw on a large stock of 'trust capital', an often formidable reputation and a safety net of deep-rooted public support, if not devotion. If I may take the example of the Bundesbank, the borderline between trust and quasi-religious faith is certainly very hard to distinguish. Jacques Delors is said to have once remarked: 'Not all Germans believe in God, but all believe in the Bundesbank.' Such a degree of faith is, of course, partly the result of the success that this central bank had in maintaining its promise of stable money. However, one needs to remember that the Bundesbank (and its predecessor, the Bank Deutscher Länder) started from almost nothing after the catastrophes of tyranny, war and inflation, which had thoroughly destroyed faith and trust in public authority. In this regard the ECB, thankfully, is in a much more favourable position.

The attitude of the German public towards their central bank is also the product of the high premium that was – and continues to be – placed on stability in Germany, as a consequence of the traumatic instabilities of war and inflation in the first half of the twentieth century, which explains this sort of 'faith' in the case of Germany. André Glucksmann has used the term 'currency religion' to describe the Germans' devotion to monetary stability and to the Bundesbank as the guardian of the D-Mark.[11] In my view such devotion, nevertheless, represents something of an anomaly. I am not sure that it is necessarily always helpful for an institution like a central bank to be held in such awe. Central bankers rightly become nervous – or at least slightly uncomfortable – if public expectations become too high or are elevated to quasi-religious dimensions. Moreover, if a central bank – for whatever reasons – acquires prestige and standing that transcends the strict confines of its mandate, and becomes an object of faith or mythical devotion, this may suggest that it fills a void left elsewhere. In particular this may be an indication of a lack of confidence in other – principally more important – institutions in society.

To my mind independent central banks fulfil an important function for the benefit of society. Their job is to maintain price stability, trust and confidence in the currency. Nothing more and nothing less should be asked of them. This reflects a clean division of labour and a clear allocation of responsibilities vis-à-vis other economic policy actors and, especially, vis-à-vis democratically elected governments. Stable money is too important to be overburdened with other purposes. This is especially important in the process of European integration.

Faith in the European Central Bank, faith in Europe?

The move to European Monetary Union is an important step in the long history of closer European integration. In particular, in the field of monetary policy the Maastricht Treaty represents a

---

11   A. Glucksmann, 'Lieber die Mark als noch einmal Hitler', *Rheinischer Merkur*, 3 September 1993.

decisive act of delegation of decision-making authority or sovereignty. The Treaty entrusts the objective of price stability to an independent and supranational body, the European Central Bank.

The Treaty was ratified by the parliaments and governments of all Member States of the European Union and in some cases endorsed by referendum. Thus the delegation of European monetary policy to the ECB is endowed with full democratic legitimacy. This bond of legitimacy is a crucial aspect of sound institutional foundations for monetary policy. There is no doubt that in order to be successful over the longer term, the ECB as the guardian of price stability – like any institution in a democracy – will have to win and maintain the trust and support of the European public. It can and should be held accountable for fulfilling its mandate. This mandate is clear, but it is also limited. It needs to be understood what monetary policy can be expected to deliver, but also what it *cannot* be expected to achieve.

This is particularly important in the case of the European Monetary Union, which not only delegates the authority for monetary policy to an independent central bank but also severs the traditionally close link between the currency and the nation state. Historically, currency jurisdictions and national borders have tended to coincide, at least in more recent times. This reflects the fact that the right to issue money has been seen as a key attribute of national sovereignty. Thus monetary union cannot be regarded as just a small and innocuous step of a primarily technical nature. One is hard pressed to find examples in history where sovereign nation states voluntarily chose to cede or share sovereignty in the monetary field. It is therefore clear that European economic and monetary union has been and will continue to be part of the wider

economic and political project that the process of European integration has represented from the very start.

Monetary union is certainly not only about money. It is an important element in the very successful quest for lasting peace, stability and prosperity in Europe. This quest involves the building of
trust and the sharing of sovereignty among European partners and
the building of common institutions, in cases where this is desirable for the benefit of all. Europe is more than a collection of nation states, but it also stops far short of becoming a single federal
entity. I do not believe that a stable monetary regime necessarily
must have its root at the level of the nation state. Going back in history, the international gold standard coincided with an era of stability. It was a system that was fundamentally based on rules and
which transcended the nation state. Nevertheless, as a currency
that is new and not linked in the traditional way to the nation state
the euro does face particular challenges in winning the trust and
the hearts of the people.

Money is clearly regarded as more than simply a medium of
exchange or a unit of account. It is a symbol to which people are
attached in meta-economical – if not religious – terms. The Arch-
bishop of Canterbury, George Carey, once stated: 'I want the
Queen's head on the bank notes. The point about national identity is very important. I don't want to become French or German.' Personally, I do not feel less German because I share a
currency with fellow Europeans, just as presumably the Welsh,
for example, can retain a strong sense of identity despite sharing
the same money with the English. I also believe that a European
identity – with its own shared symbols and characteristics – can
happily co-exist with, and even reinforce, national, regional and
local identities. Nevertheless, symbols matter. The euro reflects

the economic reality that now binds together those countries that have adopted it as their currency. It will also inevitably be regarded as a broader symbol of a shared future and destiny.

Whatever the wider goals and ambitions of European integration may be, one thing is clear. The first and foremost objective of European Monetary Union was not simply to create a *common* currency but also a *stable* currency. This is the promise that Europe needs to fulfil on a lasting basis. A stable money is too important to be regarded just as an instrument for other political ambitions. The reverse is true: without stable money all further ambition will come to nothing. Jacques Rueff famously claimed in 1950 that 'Europe will be built on money or it will not be built'. I would contend that European integration in the meantime had progressed quite successfully even without a single currency. Now that the step to monetary union has been taken – and only now – I can, however, fully subscribe to his statement. You will probably understand that I would, however, add an adjective: 'Europe will be built on *stable* money or it will not be built'.

The prime minister of Portugal, Antonio Guterres, is reported in 1995 to have taken this line one step farther. He drew the analogy with Jesus' call on St Peter when founding the Christian Church: 'Thou art Peter, the rock, and on this rock I shall build my church' turned into 'Thou art the euro, on this new currency shall we build our Europe'.[12] I must admit I would prefer to make the argument in more secular terms and not to overburden the euro with additional hopes, beliefs or visions. Fulfilling the promise of a stable money – taken by itself – is not a trivial requirement, but it is not a matter of faith in the religious sense as discussed at the be-

---

12   Reported in the *Frankfurter Allgemeine Zeitung*, 13 December 1995.

ginning of my speech. The practical task of maintaining price stability, of preserving the value of the new currency, the euro, falls to the European Central Bank. The ECB is well equipped to do its job. At the same time other policy-makers in Europe also have to play their part.

Concluding remarks

Should we have faith in central banks? My first answer to this question was a clear 'no' if faith means 'belief in unquestioned authority'. Central bankers should not ask just for faith, they cannot expect such faith, and they cannot take faith for granted. Instead they must work hard every day to earn the trust that the public places in them. Central bankers are not superhuman; they cannot be guaranteed to be benevolent or omniscient. They will perform best within an institution that is given a clear objective and that is held accountable by the public.

Conversely, the public would be ill advised to put 'blind trust' in central bankers. Price stability, preserving the value of money, is the pre-condition for a well-functioning market economy, for economic and social stability, a free and prosperous society. Price stability is too important to society to be left 'on trust' to the vagaries of the political process or to the whims of individual central bankers. It requires the building of solid and strong independent institutions that are dedicated to serving and defending the common good of price stability.

It is both economically sensible as well as democratically legitimate for society to delegate such a limited and well-defined task to an independent central bank. Such an act of delegation confers an obligation on the central bank to fulfil this trust and to be held accountable. Faith may be all right, but control by an attentive public will also be needed. On the second meaning of 'faith', in the sense of a justified belief, a well-founded expectation, I believe there are good reasons for trusting independent central banks with the maintenance of price stability.

Finally, trust can be regarded as a stock of capital or 'credit' that is built up in the relationship between the central bank and its ultimate master, the public it serves. Such a stock of trust is the basis for keeping faith in difficult times. Trust flows in both directions and – like stable money – it is a common good. Trust breeds more trust in return. But the building of trust in a relationship requires some time and patience.

The importance of trust has recently been stressed in a statement on the euro by European bishops. They write: 'As Bishops, we are theologians and pastors, as well as, of course, citizens of our own countries and of Europe. Irrespective of how we approach the subject of "the euro and monetary union", we always reach the same basic consideration: that where currencies are concerned, reliability and stability constitute essential conditions for ensuring trust and confidence ... Without trust, a currency cannot maintain a stable value. This applies particularly to the European currency, of which the creation and development is unprecedented in history.'[13]

I believe that the European Central Bank can take credit and, indeed, pride in achieving its mandate so far. Its mandate is the maintenance of price stability in the euro area over the medium

---

13 Commission of the Bishops' Conferences of the European Community (COMECE), *A Stable Monetary Union – Hope for a Europe of Solidarity*, statement by the bishops of COMECE two years after the introduction of the euro, Brussels, 6 December 2000.

term. Nothing more and nothing less. There can be no doubt that the ECB is determined and committed to continuing to fulfil its responsibility and keeping the promise of a stable currency for Europe. This commitment is the basis for earning the trust and confidence of the public, the citizens, the people we serve.

Should we fail in the pursuit of this task the statutes of the ECB may not provide for any immediate sanctions or material punishment. As mentioned before, I would not regard such sanctions as either necessary or effective. However, central bankers may well take fright from a glance at Dante's *Divina Commedia*. There, a certain Adam of Brescia is mentioned, guilty of the crime of falsifying coins – that is, creating inflation. His punishment in one of the darkest – or rather hottest – corners of hell is a horribly inflated belly. Central bankers beware!

COMMENTARY

GEOFFREY E. WOOD

In his fascinating lecture Professor Issing returns to a subject he has touched on – albeit from a different perspective – before. In 1995 he spoke at City University, London, on 'Ethics and Morals in Central Banking – Do They Exist? Do They Matter?'[1] There he considered '... how far and in what way ethical and moral aspects could, or perhaps even should, play a role in central bank policy'.

Many economists have argued they should play no role. Binding rules should replace discretion. The 'rule by men'[2] should be replaced by 'rule by law'.[3]

In his classic 'Rules versus Authorities in Monetary Policy',[4] Henry Simons set out the case for established rules superseding discretion. The principles guiding their choice, he wrote, should be as follows:

> In a free-enterprise system we obviously need highly definite
> and stable rules of the game, especially as to money. The

1   O. Issing, 'Ethics and Morals in Central Banking – Do They Exist? Do They Matter?', in Forrest Capie and Geoffrey E. Wood (eds), *Monetary Economics in the 1990s*, Macmillan, 1996.

2   M. Friedman, 'Should there be an Independent Monetary Authority?', in L.B.Yeager (ed.), *In Search of a Monetary Constitution*, Cambridge, Mass., 1962.

3   F.A. Hayek, *Die Verfassung der Freiheit* (The Constitution of Freedom), Tübingen, 1971.

4   H.C. Simons, 'Rules versus Authorities in Monetary Policy', reprint in Simons, *Economic Policy for a Free Society*, Chicago, 1948.

monetary rules must be compatible with the reasonably smooth working of the system. Once established, however, they should work mechanically, with the chips falling where they may. To put our present problem as a paradox – we need to design and establish with the greatest intelligence a monetary system good enough so that hereafter, we may hold to it unrationally – on faith – as a religion, if you please.

To assure adequate moral pressure of public opinion against legislative (and administrative) tinkering, the monetary rules must be definite, simple (at least in principle), and expressive of strong, abiding, pervasive, and reasonably popular sentiments. They should be designed to permit the fullest and most stable employment, to facilitate adjustment to such basic changes (especially in technology) as are likely to occur, and, secondarily, to minimise inequities between debtors and creditors.

These two quotations, taken together, state the ethical case for rules rather than discretion and set out both ethical and efficiency arguments for a particular rule. Professor Issing endorses the aim and accepts the arguments. Both equity between borrowers and lenders and economic efficiency (actually inseparable from borrower-lender equity) require stable prices, or at least an approximation to them, and that is the aim of monetary policy that Professor Issing supports.

I share that aim. In this commentary, therefore, I shall take the aim as given and touch on several other matters. First, on why the best we can hope for is an approximation to price stability, rather than price stability itself; second, I shall link Professor Issing's arguments to some arguments in moral philosophy and in mathematical economics; and third, I shall relate the arguments to an important duty of a central bank that is not mentioned in Professor Issing's paper.

Why an approximation?

Many but not all central banks nowadays have an explicit target for inflation. The ECB has a target of inflation remaining below 2 per cent p.a. over the medium term; the Bank of England has a target of 1.5 to 3.5 per cent p.a. Neither of these is a target for a stable price level. A target of this sort would require that any rise in the price level, however modest, would have to be reversed. Even the ECB's target does not require, or indeed permit, that; the ECB has stressed time and again that its target is symmetric in the sense that it excludes deflation as well as inflation.

Various arguments have been advanced as to why it is beneficial for real output growth to allow a steady, albeit gentle, decline in the purchasing power of money; these have been surveyed thoroughly and critically in a paper by William Poole, President of the Federal Reserve Bank of St Louis. Even if one concludes that neither theory nor evidence can justify ever-rising prices, there remains a difficulty with choosing a stable price level target. The problem is one of measurement. Every year there is technical change. This leads to changes, quite often improvements, in the quality of goods – notably in the case of consumer durables – and over a period of years can lead to the vanishing, at any rate for all practical purposes, of some goods from general consumption. Very few of us now work by candlelight and travel to and from work on horseback. The improvement and displacement of goods create problems for the construction of price indices. When electric light displaced candles, it may at first have been more expensive, or it may not. Either way there was an enormous change in the quality of light supplied. The same is true with improving goods. The good may have the same name, but the quality of it, and hence the use one gets in exchange for a given amount of money, changes. How can we allow for that? Allowance is difficult and inevitably depends partly on judgement. Caution probably leads to an understatement of the benefits of these changes. For that reason it is usually accepted that a *low* rate of *measured* inflation approximates to stable prices.

How low? This section started with a comparison of the inflation targets of the ECB and the Bank of England. Most economists and statisticians would agree that anything above the Bank of England's target is not 'low', using that term in the sense of the present discussion.

But the central point is that we inevitably have to aim at an approximation to price stability. That is where faith first comes in. Not in the case of the Bank of England (for its target was chosen by a government, so it had no role in the choice), but certainly in the case of the ECB. The Maastricht Treaty has given the ECB a clear mandate, namely maintaining price stability. On the basis of this mandate the ECB has announced the definitions mentioned above.

All those who use its currency have to have faith that the target chosen is a good approximation to price stability. Or, to look at the other side of the coin, ethics and morality are in this task inseparable from the duties of a central banker – a point Professor Issing argued in his above-cited lecture.[5]

---

5   Issing, op. cit.

Philosophy and game theory

The virtues of a market economy have been argued from several viewpoints. Adam Smith summarised one argument in what has become the most famous quotation in all economics: 'It is not from the benevolence of the butcher, the brewer or the baker that we expect our dinner, but from their regard to their own interest. We address ourselves, not to their humanity but to their self-love.'[6]

The interaction of all sorts of producers, responding to signals from the market as to what will yield them the highest profit, produces what consumers want. The 'invisible hand' (again a phrase from Smith) coordinates the use of our productive resources so as to produce what we desire.

The market, then, is efficient. It is also moral – it limits government, by limiting its domain, and thus helps protect against the 'tyranny of the majority' – an important task, as John Stuart Mill argued compellingly in 'On Liberty'.

Markets are nevertheless imperfect. If people are going to transact only once, the incentive to cheat is high. The famous 'prisoners' dilemma' illustrates this. Two men are arrested; each is told that they may be convicted of a serious or a minor charge. There is sufficient evidence to convict on the latter, which will produce one year in jail. An incentive can be offered; implicate the other, and go free. The implicated will get a ten-year sentence. If both inform, they will get five years each. The pursuit of self-interest is plainly sub-optimal; cooperation (if it is possible) produces the shortest sentence.

Hence there is sometimes a case for cooperation rather than competition. If the game is played over and over, the prisoners

---

6   Adam Smith, *An Inquiry into the Nature and Causes of the Wealth of Nations*, 1776.

come to realise that non-cooperation harms both. In the market, the likelihood of repeated transactions ensures honest dealing.

So, the market is good, and it should be used *repeatedly* – and not just locally, but over a wide range. Without money there is only barter, which greatly restricts the range and frequency of trading, for barter is expensive in time and effort.[7] Money is needed for the market to work in delivering efficient and moral outcomes. But not any money. As the value of money becomes less predictable, prices quoted in terms of money become less and less meaningful. High inflation can drive people back to barter – this has happened in the hyper-inflations of the past, when inflation rates have risen in some cases to over 10,000 per cent p.a. Growth has stopped and societies have collapsed under these circumstances. More modest inflations have – in Latin America, for example – sometimes led to dictatorships, initially attempting to restore economic order. And even modest inflation harms growth – Robert Barro has written some fascinating studies showing this.

So to conclude on this, then, the arguments for central banks aiming at a good approximation for price stability are compelling; and if they are allowed to choose their own target, we can only have faith that it will be well chosen.

But even if a bank has its target chosen for it, faith in the bank is required, for the specification of the target is inevitably incomplete. Take as an example the Bank of England. Suppose inflation goes outside the target range. How fast should the Bank get it back in? One would expect that the faster it did so, the bigger the temporary effect on output, and possibly the bigger the risk of shoot-

---

7   A. Meltzer, 'What is Money', in *Money, Prices, and the Real Economy*, ed. G.E. Wood, Edward Elgar, Cheltenham, 1998; F.H. Capie and G.E. Wood, 'E-money, lender of last resort, and the role of the central bank', forthcoming.

ing out the other side of the target. One has to trust the Bank to return at a sensible rate. What is sensible is not an easy question, any more than achieving the chosen rate is an easy task; but it must surely be a rate such that the output effects do not cause discontent with the notion of having a target for inflation.

And of course, if a central bank – the US Federal Reserve is a good example – has a range of targets so wide as to incorporate almost any policy course, one can only have faith that it will choose sensibly.

The other task

Central banks must have at least two tasks. Maintaining monetary stability is one. Maintaining what is called, in the latest Bank of England Act, financial stability is the other.

What is financial stability, and how is it to be maintained?

The meaning can be drawn broadly or narrowly. A narrow sense involves providing liquidity to the banking system in an emergency, so as to maintain the stability of that system. A broader sense would require the central bank to stabilise a range of asset markets. Those who urge the broader task do not, however, exclude the first; they add to it. In the present discussion, focus is on the first, narrower and uncontentious, task.

It evolved in the nineteenth century in Britain (although the necessity of it was recognised late in the eighteenth century). The great names in the development of the notion of the central bank acting as 'lender of last resort' (LOLR) are Henry Thornton and Walter Bagehot. The argument is in its essence very simple. Banks maintain only a small fraction of what is deposited with them as cash or as immediately realisable assets. If a bank fails, doubts arise about others, there are demands for cash, and if they cannot be met then the failure of one bank can lead to the collapse of a major part of the system. Just such a chain of events was the overwhelmingly important cause of the Great Depression in the United States.

The lender of last resort prevents this by lending freely on securities whenever there is a scramble for cash. The demand for cash is thus satisfied, there are no waves of bank failures, and the system survives. This is a vital duty. A central bank can be instructed to act thus whenever a crisis comes. But it must be trusted to act quickly and with sufficient vigour. No rigid set of rules, apart from the general rule enjoining LOLR action, is possible, for not all crises are exactly alike with exactly the same warning signals and course of events.

One has to have faith that central banks will act properly. Again, the faith has to depend on a sensible structure, allowing LOLR action; and the faith will be grounded in past performance. This grounding in past performance can be seen to have consequences. Deposit insurance was introduced in the USA in the 1930s as a way of preventing panic scrambles for cash, because the Federal Reserve had failed to avert the consequences of such a scramble only a few years before. In contrast, when deposit protection was introduced in the UK, it was certainly not intended to preserve the stability of the banking system, for the Bank of England had shown that it could do that very well. Rather it was simply intended to protect the savings of those with little wealth.

Conclusion

Otmar Issing asks 'Should we have faith in central banks?' As he argues, and as the above comments have supported him in arguing, such faith is inevitable, for the rules that might appear to make it unnecessary can never be so detailed as to make some measure of trust, or confidence, or faith – whatever word one uses – unnecessary. This faith must, of course, be grounded both on a sensible central bank structure, and on experience. It should not be blind. That helps explain why central banks are traditionally cautious. One mistake can do great damage to a reputation for competence. Reputation is hard to establish but easy to destroy.

In his lecture, Otmar Issing has opened up discussion of the relationship between a central bank's constitution and its policies in a novel, fascinating and important way. His lecture will give rise to much further discussion and work.

ABOUT THE IEA

The Institute is a research and educational charity (No. CC 235 351), limited by guarantee. Its mission is to improve understanding of the fundamental institutions of a free society with particular reference to the role of markets in solving economic and social problems.

The IEA achieves its mission by:

- a high-quality publishing programme
- conferences, seminars, lectures and other events
- outreach to school and college students
- brokering media introductions and appearances

The IEA, which was established in 1955 by the late Sir Antony Fisher, is an educational charity, not a political organisation. It is independent of any political party or group and does not carry on activities intended to affect support for any political party or candidate in any election or referendum, or at any other time. It is financed by sales of publications, conference fees and voluntary donations.

In addition to its main series of publications the IEA also publishes a quarterly journal, *Economic Affairs*, and has two specialist programmes – Environment and Technology, and Education.

The IEA is aided in its work by a distinguished international Academic Advisory Council and an eminent panel of Honorary Fellows. Together with other academics, they review prospective IEA publications, their comments being passed on anonymously to authors. All IEA papers are therefore subject to the same rigorous independent refereeing process as used by leading academic journals.

IEA publications enjoy widespread classroom use and course adoptions in schools and universities. They are also sold throughout the world and often translated/reprinted.

Since 1974 the IEA has helped to create a world-wide network of 100 similar institutions in over 70 countries. They are all independent but share the IEA's mission.

Views expressed in the IEA's publications are those of the authors, not those of the Institute (which has no corporate view), its Managing Trustees, Academic Advisory Council members or senior staff.

Members of the Institute's Academic Advisory Council, Honorary Fellows, Trustees and Staff are listed on the following page.

The Institute gratefully acknowledges financial support for its publications programme and other work from a generous benefaction by the late Alec and Beryl Warren.

The Institute of Economic Affairs
2 Lord North Street, Westminster, London SW1P 3LB
Tel: 020 7799 8900
Fax: 020 7799 2137
Email: iea@iea.org.uk
Internet: iea.org.uk

Other papers recently published by the IEA include:

WHO, What and Why?
Transnational Government, Legitimacy and the World Health Organization
Roger Scruton
Occasional Paper 113; ISBN 0 255 36487 3
£8.00

The World Turned Rightside Up
A New Trading Agenda for the Age of Globalisation
John C. Hulsman
Occasional Paper 114; ISBN 0 255 36495 4
£8.00

The Representation of Business in English Literature
Introduced and edited by Arthur Pollard
Readings 53; ISBN 0 255 36491 1
£12.00

Anti-Liberalism 2000
The Rise of New Millennium Collectivism
David Henderson
Occasional Paper 115; ISBN 0 255 36497 0
£7.50

Capitalism, Morality and Markets

Brian Griffiths, Robert A. Sirico, Norman Barry & Frank Field
Readings 54; ISBN 0 255 36496 2
£7.50

A Conversation with Harris and Seldon

Ralph Harris & Arthur Seldon
Occasional Paper 116; ISBN 0 255 36498 9
£7.50

Malaria and the DDT Story

Richard Tren & Roger Bate
Occasional Paper 117; ISBN 0 255 36499 7
£10.00

A Plea to Economists Who Favour Liberty: Assist the Everyman

Daniel B. Klein
Occasional Paper 118; ISBN 0 255 36501 2
£10.00

Waging the War of Ideas

John Blundell
Occasional Paper 119; ISBN 0 255 36500 4
£10.00

The Changing Fortunes of Economic Liberalism

Yesterday, Today and Tomorrow
David Henderson
Occasional Paper 105 (new edition); ISBN 0 255 36520 9
£12.50

The Global Education Industry

Lessons from Private Education in Developing Countries
James Tooley
Hobart Paper 141 (new edition); ISBN 0 255 36503 9
£12.50

Saving Our Streams

The Role of the Anglers' Conservation Association in
Protecting English and Welsh Rivers
Roger Bate
Research Monograph 53; ISBN 0 255 36494 6
£10.00

Better Off Out?

The Benefits or Costs of EU Membership
Brian Hindley & Martin Howe
Occasional Paper 99 (new edition); ISBN 0 255 36502 0
£10.00

Buckingham at 25

Freeing the Universities from State Control
Edited by James Tooley
Readings 55; ISBN 0 255 36512 8
£15.00

Lectures on Regulatory and Competition Policy

Irwin M. Stelzer
Occasional Paper 120; ISBN 0 255 36511 X
£12.50

Misguided Virtue

False Notions of Corporate Social Responsibility
David Henderson
Hobart Paper 142; ISBN 0 255 36510 1
£12.50

HIV and Aids in Schools

The Political Economy of Pressure Groups and Miseducation
Barrie Craven, Pauline Dixon, Gordon Stewart & James Tooley
Occasional Paper 121; ISBN 0 255 36522 5
£10.00

The Road to Serfdom

The Reader's Digest *condensed version*
Friedrich A. Hayek
Occasional Paper 122; ISBN 0 255 36530 6
£7.50

Bastiat's *The Law*

Introduction by Norman Barry
Occasional Paper 123; ISBN 0 255 36509 8
£7.50

A Globalist Manifesto for Public Policy

Charles Calomiris
Occasional Paper 124; ISBN 0 255 36525 X
£7.50

Euthanasia for Death Duties

Putting Inheritance Tax Out of Its Misery
Barry Bracewell-Milnes
Research Monograph 54; ISBN 0 255 36513 6
£10.00

Liberating the Land

The Case for Private Land-use Planning
Mark Pennington
Hobart Paper 143; ISBN 0 255 36508 x
£10.00

IEA Yearbook of Government Performance 2002/2003

Edited by Peter Warburton
Yearbook 1; ISBN 0 255 36532 2
£15.00

Britain's Relative Economic Performance, 1870–1999

Nicholas Crafts
Research Monograph 55; ISBN 0 255 36524 1
£10.00

To order copies of currently available IEA papers, or to enquire about availability, please contact:

Lavis Marketing
73 Lime Walk
Oxford OX3 7AD

Tel: 01865 767575
Fax: 01865 750079
Email: orders@lavismarketing.co.uk

The IEA also offers a subscription service to its publications. For a single annual payment, currently £40.00 in the UK, you will receive every title the IEA publishes across the course of a year, invitations to events, and discounts on our extensive back catalogue. For more information, please contact:

Subscriptions
The Institute of Economic Affairs
2 Lord North Street
London SW1P 3LB

Tel: 020 7799 8900
Fax: 020 7799 2137
Website: www.iea.org.uk